Stella's Bright Ideas

Story by Aleesah Darlison
Illustrations by Emma Trithart

Stella's Bright Ideas

Text: Aleesah Darlison
Publishers: Tania Mazzeo and Eliza Webb
Series consultant: Amanda Sutera
 Hands on Heads Consulting
Editor: Kirsty Hine
Project editor: Annabel Smith
Designer: Jess Kelly
Project designer: Danielle Maccarone
Illustrations: Emma Trithart
Production controller: Renee Tome

NovaStar

ISBN 978 0 17 033433 4

Cengage Learning Australia
Level 5, 80 Dorcas Street
Southbank VIC 3006 Australia
Phone: 1300 790 853
Email: aust.nelsonprimary@cengage.com

For learning solutions, visit **cengage.com.au**

Printed in China by 1010 Printing International Ltd
1 2 3 4 5 6 7 28 27 26 25 24

*Nelson acknowledges the Traditional Owners and Custodians
of the lands of all First Nations Peoples. We pay respect
to Elders past and present, and extend that respect to
all First Nations Peoples today.*

Contents

Chapter 1

The Lost Dog

Stella loved solving problems. Mum called Stella her "ideas girl". Whenever Stella had an idea to solve a problem, a light went on in her brain. Her mind raced with thoughts. Possibilities. Solutions.

Stella also loved helping animals, especially dogs. She would have loved a dog of her own, but her family lived in a small house with a small yard on the edge of town. Both her parents worked, and Dad said they didn't have time to train a dog. But that didn't stop Stella from wanting one. Or from wanting to pat every dog she saw.

One cold autumn afternoon, Stella was walking home from school with Dad and her little brother, Finn, when she saw a dog wandering alone on the street.

"Look!" Stella pointed at the small brown dog. "That dog is out by itself."

"Maybe it's lost," said Finn.

"It's wearing a collar," Stella said. She stepped closer to the dog. It was shivering, and its fur had been cut short.

"Careful, it might bite," Dad warned.

Stella reached out a hand to the dog. It licked her. "It's friendly. And it's cold." She giggled as the dog licked her hand again while she was checking its collar. "There's a phone number on the tag. Can we call the owner, Dad?"

"Sure," Dad said, retrieving his phone from his pocket.

"His name is Buster," Stella said. When she said the dog's name, Buster licked her yet again. "Come on, boy. Let's get you back to your home."

Chapter 2

A Bright Idea

Stella and Dad soon found the address the dog's owner had given Dad on the phone. Stella followed Dad and Finn through the open gate. They had to step around toy cars and balls.

Stella knocked on the door.

A woman appeared holding a crying toddler. When she saw Buster, her eyes lit up. "Thank you so much for bringing him home. Max needed his nappy changed when we got back from the shops so I was rushing to get inside. I must have left the gate open, and Buster got out. I'm Helen." Dad introduced everyone and explained that Stella had found Buster.

The little dog looked happy to be home, but he was still shivering.

"I think Buster might be cold," Stella said.

"I think you're right," Helen said, sighing.
"I've been so busy with Max that I haven't
been able to look after Buster properly.
I thought if I got his fur trimmed he
would need less grooming. But it's been
so cold lately."

"At least he's home now," Dad said.
"We'd better go – come on, kids."

"Thanks again," Helen said. "Feel free
to visit Buster whenever you like," she told
Stella. "He could do with someone else to
play with."

As Stella left with Dad and Finn, she
thought: *I need a bright idea to help Buster.*

The answer came to Stella that night as she was putting her pyjamas on after her shower. "I've got it!" she cried.

Stella asked Mum if she could use the computer to do some research on the internet. She searched for "dog coat knitting patterns". Several images came up.

"It has to be simple," Stella murmured as she scanned the images. She kept scrolling until she came to a blue-and-white striped pattern that looked easy to make. But when she checked the craft cupboard, there wasn't any wool.

That's when Stella had her second bright idea.

Chapter 3

Woolly Work

On Saturday, Stella searched the shelves of wool at the op shop until she found the colours she needed. She carried the wool and two knitting needles to the counter.

"Is that all you need?" Mum asked.

"Yes, I'm only making one coat, and Buster is small." Stella had brought her pocket money. Luckily, the wool and needles didn't cost much.

When Stella got home, she set to work using the knitting pattern she had found on the internet. She made some mistakes but she stuck with it, determined to finish the coat for Buster.

The next day, Stella rode her bike to Buster's house. Helen and Max were playing with Buster in the front yard. Buster was happy to see Stella, but he was still shivering.

"I knitted Buster a coat," Stella told Helen. "Can I try it on him?"

"Of course," Helen said. "What a wonderful idea!"

Buster looked pleased with his new coat.

"Hello!" a voice called from the other side of the fence.

"Stella, this is Stavros, my neighbour," Helen said.

"What a lovely dog coat," Stavros said. "Did you make it?"

Stella blushed. "Yes."

Stavros held up a small black poodle. "This is Rex. He's rather old so he feels the cold. Could you knit him a coat, too? I'd pay you."

Stella wasn't sure her knitting was good enough to be paid money for, but Stavros insisted.

Later that day, when Stella told Mum about Stavros's request, Mum said, "I'll grab my car keys."

"What for?" Stella asked.

Mum laughed. "So we can buy more wool from the op shop, of course!"

Stella picked out some new colours for Rex. This coat would have red and white stripes. When Stella, Mum and Finn delivered it to Stavros later that week, he was so happy with the coat that he took a photo of Rex wearing it. Then he posted the photo on social media, tagging it with "#cosycoat".

@King_Rex

Rex looking handsome in his new #cosycoat

Stavros's phone dinged. People were already commenting on his post. "Two of my friends want to buy coats for their dogs," he said.

Stella nodded. "Okay."

"How wonderful. Give them my phone number so we can arrange their orders," Mum told Stavros.

As they walked home from Stavros's, house, Stella was struck with another bright idea. "I might be able to start a business making these dog coats," she said. "There must be lots of dogs in town that need to keep warm during winter."

"What will you do with the money you earn?" Mum asked.

Finn gave Stella a cheeky grin. "You could give it to me."

"Very funny," Stella said. "I'm not sure what I'll save up for, but it'll be something special. Something important."

Stella thought about it all the way home. *I need another bright idea.*

Chapter 4

Cosy Coats

Stella spent the afternoon helping Dad set up a website and a social media page. She called her business "Cosy Coats". Then Mum created a bank account and a spreadsheet to track her sales and her costs.

Stella bought more wool and asked Finn to help her knit some coats. Helen and Stavros sent photos of their dogs modelling their cosy coats, which Dad helped Stella post on social media.

Stella soon received more orders from family, friends and new customers. She spent her spare time looking for new knitting patterns and researching community groups she could donate the money she earned to.

A few weeks later, when Stella was on her way home from school, she saw a poster advertising the local markets. That's when she had another bright idea.

That night, Stella spoke to her parents about having a stall at the market.

"What a great idea!" Mum said.

Saturday soon arrived. The whole family helped pack the cosy coats into the car, then set out to Fig Tree Park.

Stella was nervous. "Do you think we'll sell any coats?" She had spent hours knitting during the week, and she really wanted to make sure the dogs in town were warm in winter.

Dad shrugged. "We'll have to wait and see."

At the markets, Stella, Mum, Dad and Finn set up their stall. It wasn't long before a man with two dogs approached. "Cosy Coats!" he gasped. "I've seen these online. Fitzroy! Fergus! We simply must buy some coats for you!"

After that, everyone wanted a cosy coat. Stella couldn't believe it when she sold out of everything.

The family shared a group hug. "Let's have some dumplings to celebrate," Dad said.

As she wandered through the market eating dumplings, Stella saw a stall for Puppy Paws Dog Shelter. Several flyers showed photos of lovable dogs looking for homes. To one side of the stall, there were three pups in a small, fenced area. Plenty of people passed by, but no one stopped to talk to the stallholders.

Except Stella.

"Hi, I'm Stella."

"I'm Asha," the stallholder said. "This is my husband, Don."

"I knit cosy coats for dogs," Stella explained. "Do the dogs at your shelter need coats for winter?"

"Some do," Asha said, "but more than that, they need homes. That's why we're at the market. We're looking for donations to help run the shelter, and we need people to adopt the dogs in our care."

Don smiled. "We love seeing dogs find forever homes."

Stella felt sad for the dogs that needed a home. She took a flyer from the table and walked back to her parents.

What can I do to help? she wondered. *I need another bright idea.*

Chapter 5

A Big Problem

"This problem is too big for me to solve on my own," Stella said, as she stood at the front of her classroom the following Monday. "That's why I'm asking for your help. Please join my knitting club so we can make more cosy coats and sell them to raise money for the dogs at Puppy Paws Dog Shelter. Thank you."

Mr Ruffley, Stella's teacher, applauded along with her classmates.

"I'll join your knitting club!" Amar called.

"Me too!" Alex said.

"Me three!" Lily added.

"I can't knit," Kartik said, "but we have wool at home we can donate."

Stella smiled. Asking for help had been another bright idea.

Kids from different classes joined Stella's knitting club and were soon knitting up a storm. Mr Ruffley helped Stella and her friends create a fun video about the cosy coats and how they were raising money to help Puppy Paws Dog Shelter. Then he emailed everyone's parents asking them to upload the video to their social media pages. The video got hundreds of views. Orders for cosy coats flowed in.

※ Puppy Paws Dog Shelter
※ Cosy Coats

Stella saved the money from selling cosy coats and kept it in her bank account. For several weeks, she continued going to the markets every Saturday. Sometimes her friends from school helped on the stall.

Chapter 6

The Shelter

Stella had soon saved enough money.
She was ready.

With Mr Ruffley's help, Stella organised
a class excursion to Puppy Paws Dog
Shelter. The students would learn about
dog shelters and caring for pets, and they
would be there to see Stella announce her
big donation.

Dad helped Stella make a post to put on
social media, inviting local dog lovers to
attend the event as well.

When Stella and her classmates stepped
off the bus, a crowd of people had already
gathered. Lots of dog owners were there.
Many of their pets wore Stella's cosy coats.

"Stella!" Asha called, as she and Don hurried over to her. "I can't believe you organised this all by yourself."

"The idea was mine," Stella admitted, "but I had help to make today happen. When everyone heard the shelter needed support, we all worked together. Mum and Dad helped me a lot. My brother and my friends in the knitting club pitched in to donate wool and make cosy coats. And my teacher, Mr Ruffley, helped out too."

Don shook his head in wonder. "We've never had this many people visit. There are loads of them inside wanting to adopt dogs."

"That's fantastic!" Stella said. "And we made so much money from making cosy coats that we want to give it to you to help run the shelter. We'll be able to donate more each month as we sell more coats."

Asha gave Stella a hug. People in the crowd took photos.

Stella smiled as she watched dogs from the shelter being led outside by their new owners. She couldn't believe how far her bright ideas had spread. How much good they had achieved.

All from knitting a coat for a lost dog.

@puppypaws_dogshelter

#cosy coats

"We're so proud of you," Mum said, as she and Dad wandered over. "You've made a lot of dogs and people happy."

"Which is why we have a surprise for you," Dad said.

Stella's eyes lit up. "What is it?"

Finn appeared holding something small and fluffy. "Meet Lexie."

"A puppy?" Stella reached out to take the tiny dog. "We can keep her?"

"She's all ours." Mum waved the adoption papers in the air. "But she is going to need a cosy coat to keep her warm. Do you have one in her size?"

Stella grinned. "I sure do."